MW00659028

It is Often Said

Tim Hegg

"The Law Was Given to Condemn"

"The Church Replaced Israel"

"The Torah is Only for Jews"

Comments and Comparisons of Traditional Christian Theology and Hebraic Thought

Volume 4

It is Often Said

Tim Hegg

"The Law Was Given to Condemn"

"The Church Replaced Israel"

"The Torah is Only for Jews"

FIRST FRUITS OF ZION

Proclaiming the Torah and its way of life, fully centered on Messiah, to today's People of God

From a series of articles first published in *messiah magazine*

First Edition, January 2006

Printed in the United States of America

Catalog Information: Theology
CBA Category Information: BST, DOT, OTT
ISBN 1-892124-23-8

Design: Avner Wolff

First Fruits of Zion
PO Box 620099
Littleton, Colorado 80162–0099 USA
Phone (303) 933–2119 or (800) 775–4807
Fax (303) 933–0997
www.ffoz.org

Additional Study Resources

Torah Club, a monthly Torah Study Course
HaYesod, a fourteen-week Hebraic Study Course
messiah magazine

Other Books by Tim Hegg

The Letter Writer
ISBN 1-892124-16-5

Fellowheirs
ISBN 1-892124-06-8

For additional information, please visit http://www.ffoz.org

Contents

Foreword

Shalom! Thank you for purchasing *Is is Often Said, Volume 4.* We are pleased to introduce this fourth volume of Tim Hegg's articles from *messiah magazine.*

These booklets are intended to cause the body of Messiah to think through many of the common theologies of our day. This is not always an easy process. It involves letting go of preconceived ideas, opening our hearts and minds and allowing the Scriptures to define who we are.

One of these common theologies is that the Torah, God's Law, is a burden. It is a legalistic, ritualistic, archaic and condemning set of rules. This, however, is not what the Scriptures tell us. King David states that the Laws of God are perfect, sure, right, pure, clean, true and more desirable than gold (Psalm 19:7-10). Paul's statements about the Law are similar in Romans 7:12, "...the Law is holy, and the commandment is holy and righteous and good."

Many of us have had on theological glasses that have not allowed us to see the Torah through the same eyes as David and Paul. Their definitions sound very much like a description of God's character. Our common theological definition of Torah sounds more like legal list of do's and don'ts. Quite a contrast!

The Torah is indeed the character of God. It is His will and wisdom for our lives. I hope that through this series of booklets, you will come to align with David and Paul in saying that the Torah is "perfect, holy and righteous."

The Scriptures themselves should define who we are, what we think and how we live. We encourage you to get into the word for yourself. Look at the context, the historical setting and the original language. We certainly don't want you to study just for the sake of studying. Allow the Word of God to transform your heart and your mind. When you apply the truths you discover in His Word, you will truly be changed.

A rebirth is occurring among the people of God. We are watching the very fulfillment of Jeremiah 31. The Torah is being written on the hearts of men and women everywhere and we are truly coming to know Him. We desire for all of God's people to be a part of this awakening. We hope that this resource along with others will be used of God to open hearts and minds and reveal the wonderful truths in His Torah.

In Messiah,

Boaz Michael
FOUNDER, FIRST FRUITS OF ZION
WWW.FFOZ.ORG

Preface

The fear of losing Jewish identity had caused a theological shift among rabbinic Judaism of the early centuries of the Common Era. Primary in this shift was the teaching that covenant membership was based upon one's ethnic status as a Jew. And following close behind was the position that the Torah was for covenant members only, meaning only for the Jews. This necessitated a "ritual of conversion" to accommodate the Gentiles who wanted to enter the covenant. The sages ruled that the conversion ritual would give a Gentile the status of a Jew, and his children would therefore be reckoned as Jews. The "way in" for a Gentile, therefore, was through circumcision, that is, the conversion ritual.

Paul battled this deeply-embedded Jewish theology among the believers of his day. In the second chapter of Ephesians, the Apostle argues one of the central themes of his theology: the oneness of Jew and Gentile as united in Messiah. That the Gentiles should be blessed through the Abrahamic promise was never questioned; what had been left a mystery was the exact manner in which the blessing would come upon the nations. This was revealed to the Apostles and especially to Paul.[1] The method of blessing the Gentiles is emphasized by the term "fellow" used in verses 2:19 and 3:6 of Ephesians; fellow-citizens, fellow-heirs, fellow-members, fellow-partakers—they would be blessed, not in a separate community but by being grafted into the ancient community of God—the two would be wedded into one[2] and thus mutually share the blessings of God.

This teaching of the ingrafting of the Gentiles[3] was perhaps the most difficult Apostolic doctrine for the Jewish believers to accept. For centuries the Jewish nation had borne her God-ordained distinction from the nations[4] and welcomed proselytes who not only embraced the God of Abraham, Isaac, and Jacob but willingly became Jews through their proselyte ritual. The new apostolic teaching—that Gentile believers were to be accepted as full citizens within the believing community without undergoing the rituals of a proselyte—challenged the Jewish norm.[5] The Messianic community was to be a fellowship of Jew and non-Jew united in Messiah, submissive to God's Word—Yeshua (Living) and Torah (Written)—serving one another. But this issue brought division within the first-century congregations. Some apparently felt that non-Jews had fewer privileges within the community than Jews[6] and some considered full-fledged salvation impossible apart from becoming a proselyte.[7]

For Paul, each of these perspectives was ultimately a "different gospel," since union with Messiah was the sole basis of entrance and privilege within the family of God, and this union was a matter of grace. All members had the same salvific position before the Father and the same privileges of Torah life. Any gospel of salvation that taught something different than this was "anathema."[8] God accepts into His family those whose sins have been forgiven by the death of Messiah.[9] The Gentiles can be "brought near" because the dividing wall, which prohibited their coming near, was broken down through Yeshua's atoning death and resurrection. If God the Father accepts all who come by faith in Yeshua, then clearly the children ought also to accept each other. In this sense of acceptance, all the "dividing walls" of enmity—between Jew and non-Jew, man and woman, slave and free etc.—should be broken down as our minds are renewed in Him.

The foreigner (*ger*) in the Torah who attaches himself to the God of Israel, and therefore to God's people Israel, does not change his ethnic status. Yet through his faith in God and his life of obedience that this faith brings, the *ger* is given all of the privileges and responsibilities of a covenant member. And in so doing, he is a witness to the faithfulness of God in keeping His promise that "all the nations of the earth" would be blessed in Abraham. Not only is it impossible for the *ger* to change his ethnic status, it is unnecessary. For God never awarded covenant membership to anyone based upon his lineage. Covenant membership begins with God's choosing, and is secured through the faith of those He chooses.

This in no way diminishes the importance of maintaining Jewish identity in our times. God's faithfulness depends upon His promise to bless the offspring of Jacob. Yet, our essential identity is not in our ethnic status, but in our identification with Yeshua as our Messiah. The unfolding plan of redemption, given to us in the Scriptures, envisions God's covenant people as one, made up of both physical descendents of Jacob as well as those called out of the nations. What is more, this one people of God have a single focus and purpose: to please the One Who has called them by His grace, by loving Him and doing what He commands. The grand hymn of redemption has this refrain: One people, One Messiah, One Torah.

Please note, as you read through this book you will find yourself coming across terminology with which you may not be familiar. We are using the original Hebrew translation for many commonly used words because the Hebrew word gives a much fuller meaning. Yeshua is Jesus' Hebrew name. His name means "salvation." The meaning of His name alone is good reason to use it. We also use the word *Torah* when referring to the first five books of the Bible. This word means "teaching or instruction" in the Hebrew. This is a much more accurate definition of the books of Moses than the more commonly used term *law*. The word *Tanakh* is used in place of Old Testament. *Tanakh* is an acronym formed from the three sections of the Hebrew Bible—the *Torah*, the *Nevi'im* (Prophets), and the *Ketuvim* (Writings).

While the common perspective of the Torah in Christendom is that it is a millstone around the neck of mankind, the Torah itself is primarily taken up with showing Israel the means by which she could have forgiveness and right standing with God.

Is is Often Said

"The Law Was Given to Condemn"

It is amazing how perspectives change. Recently I've been going through boxes of tools that my father left me. While most of his life was taken up with teaching, preaching, and leading God's people in the truths of the Scriptures, he found great satisfaction in woodworking. And so do I. I well remember the hours that he and I spent together in the basement shop of my boyhood home. There he taught me how to use the tools and how to build with wood. I watched his patient and strong hands take plain old wood and turn it into beautiful furniture.

When I left for college, he gave me a few tools, but they only gathered dust while I spent my time doing other things. When I married and established my own home, I used the tools occasionally, but I thought the newer, more modern power tools did the job faster and better. That was 30 years ago. Now I have my own woodshop—a place where my hands and mind can work together to create and repair.

As I unpacked the boxes left to me after my father's death, the tools I sorted through were like old friends. I can even remember where they were hung in that downstairs shop. And I can still see them in my father's hands. I realize now that they are rare treasures of a bygone era when tools were made to precision and craftsmanship was the norm. But I discovered something else:

Those old hand tools still produced the finest projects if used correctly and with skill. The finely crafted square, adorned with bronze edges, is now the one I regularly reach for, because even after years of use, it has retained its absolute accurate angle. And the drawknives, made almost a century ago, have far better steel than most tools you can buy today. These tools now have a place of priority in my shop and I often reach for them first.

A Matter of Perspective

My perspective has changed because I've put these tools to the test. Over the years I've come to appreciate them more and more because their superior quality has proven itself. It's really a matter of perspective: Since I know from experience what these tools can do, I hold them in higher regard.

The matter of perspective comes into play when we read the Scriptures. Through centuries of anti-Torah theology, the "law" has come to be perceived as something bad—as something given by God to teach mankind a hard lesson. The viewpoint many have of the law is that God gave it to mankind as a kind of trap—a snare to entangle the sinner until he finally cries for help. The often-heard explanation goes like this: "God gave Israel the law because she needed to learn the lesson that she could not save herself by works. When she received the law, she immediately said to herself, 'Good! We can do this!' and set out to make her own way. However, the law was made so that it was impossible to keep. God had given Israel a trap out of which she could not escape. And so, in her attempts to keep the law, she only sank deeper and deeper into the sin of trying to keep it. The goal was that after being ensnared long enough, she would realize that the law was only given to condemn and would turn from it and receive salvation by faith. That was the message of Yeshua and His Apostles: The law condemns, so turn to God in faith and you will be free from the law."

For the majority of contemporary Bible teachers, this is the starting point for interpreting what the Bible says about the

Torah. Whenever the Torah is mentioned by the Apostles, it is interpreted with this negative perspective in mind. Granted, the Torah does have a condemning function. It reveals the righteous character of God against which all the actions of man are judged. And it rightly condemns sinners. That is one of its God-given functions. But should we presume that this is its only, or even its primary, function? Hardly! If we allow the Torah to speak for itself, we discover a different perspective. Note, for instance, Deuteronomy 30:11–14:

> For this commandment which I command you today is not too difficult for you, nor is it out of reach. It is not in heaven, that you should say, "Who will go up to heaven for us to get it for us and make us hear it, that we may observe it?" Nor is it beyond the sea, that you should say, "Who will cross the sea for us to get it for us and make us hear it, that we may observe it?" But the word is very near you, in your mouth and in your heart, that you may observe it.

In fact, the long-standing perspective of the sages is that the Torah is the supreme gift of God to His people, not some hidden trap to ensnare them. The sages state:

> Precious are Israelites, to whom was given the precious thing. It was an act of still greater love that it was made known to them that to them was given that precious thing with which the world was made, as it is said, "For I give you a good doctrine. Do not forsake my Torah" (Proverbs 4:2).[10]

> Thou art beautiful, my love (Song of Songs 1:15). "Thou art beautiful" through the commandments, both positive and negative; beautiful through loving deeds; beautiful in thy house with the heave-offerings and the tithes; beautiful in the field by the commands about gleaning the forgotten sheaf and

> the second tithe; beautiful in the law about mixed seeds and about fringes, and about first fruits, and the fourth year planting; beautiful in the law of circumcision; beautiful in prayer, in the reading of the *Shema,* in the law of the door-posts and the *tefillin,* in the law of the *lulav* and the citron; beautiful, too, in repentance and in good works; beautiful in this world and beautiful in the world to come.[11]

Contrast this with the words of Lightfoot on Galatians 3:19, where Paul asks, "Why then the Law?"

> Had the law, then, no purpose? Yes; but its very purpose, its whole character and history, betray its inferiority to the dispensation of grace. In four points this inferiority is seen. First, instead of justifying, it condemns; instead of giving life, it kills; it was added to reveal and multiply transgressions. Secondly, it was but temporary. When the seed came to whom the promise was given it was annulled. Thirdly, it did not come directly from God to man. There was a double interposition, a twofold mediation, between the giver and the recipient. There were angels who administered it as God's instruments; there was Moses (or the high-priest), who delivered it to man. Fourthly, as follows from the idea of mediation, it was of the nature of a contract, depending for its fulfillment on the observation of its conditions by the two contracting parties. Not so the promise, which, proceeding from the sole fiat of God, is unconditional and unchangeable.[12]

Two different perspectives indeed! But some might say, "Isn't this negative view of the law exactly what Paul teaches in Galatians 3:19?"

The Torah was given to reveal how God deals with transgressions among His people and how He intends to forgive them and restore the sinner to a place of fellowship.

> Why the Law then? It was added because of transgressions, having been ordained through angels by the agency of a mediator, until the seed would come to whom the promise had been made.

In the context of Galatians 3, Paul is showing that the one-sided covenant with Abraham (which he characterizes by the word *promise*), which gave unconditional blessing to the seed of Abraham, could not be overturned by the later two-sided Sinai covenant, the Torah. While those who were attempting to influence the non-Jewish Galatians were teaching that they could enter the covenant only by becoming proselytes (circumcision), Paul was arguing that the covenant made with Abraham included the nations (*goyim*); thus, their covenant membership was a matter of God's promise and grace, not something gained by submitting to the rabbinic ritual of proselytism.

The Necessity of the Torah

This left Paul with a question to answer: If covenant membership was granted by the pure grace of God's promise, what need was there for the Torah? Once a person was "in," what function did the Torah provide?

Paul's answer is straightforward: "It (the Torah) was added because of transgressions" (Galatians 3:19). As one would imagine, almost all Christian commentators interpret this statement from their predisposed negative perspective:

> ... in order that there might be transgressions, the conscious disobeying of definite commandments.[13]

> ... the purpose of the law was to increase the sum-total of transgressions.[14]

> ... for the purpose of the transgression is to be taken in a wholly negative way.[15]

However, if we seek to understand Paul's statement from a historical and grammatical perspective, an entirely different viewpoint emerges. First, Paul was a Pharisee—a Jew who had grown up learning at the feet of Gamaliel. His viewpoint of the Torah is clear: It is spiritual, holy, righteous, and good.[16] He did not think that it was a trap to ensnare Israel in sin. He was compelled to duplicate the teachings of his Master, who commissioned him as His Apostle—and Yeshua taught the enduring value of the Torah (Matthew 5:17–20).

Second, in the context of Galatians 3, Paul argues that an established covenant cannot be changed or nullified by a later covenant. Since the Torah is clearly a covenant, the argument must stand that it too has enduring, unchanging status. Third, if he were arguing that the Torah had only a negative mission and that the coming of Yeshua had done away with it, he would have fallen prey to the accusations of his detractors. Remember that when Paul arrived in Jerusalem (Acts 21), the rumor had been spread that he was teaching the abolition of the Torah. But that erroneous rumor was put to rest by his personal demonstration of Torah obedience in helping four men to complete their Nazirite vows.

What must we conclude then? That when Paul says the Torah was given "for transgressions," he is speaking of a positive function of the Torah, not a negative one. Once we change our perspective, his statement makes complete sense. The Torah was given to Israel to show how God deals with transgressions and particularly how He provides a way of forgiveness to those who are transgressors. It baffles me why the learned commentators so easily skip over the fact that the Torah is God's first clear revelation of redemption through the sacrifice of an innocent substitute. While the common perspective of the Torah in Christendom is that it is a millstone around the neck of mankind, the Torah itself is primarily taken up with showing Israel the means by which she could have forgiveness and right standing with God.

Does not Genesis begin to tell the story of redemption through substitutionary sacrifice? What else is the primary lesson of the *Akedah* (Genesis 22)[17], and what is the overarching lesson of the Joseph narrative? Consider the book of Exodus. Its whole story may be summed up in "God dwelling among His people." But how is this possible? How can God dwell among transgressors? The answer is given in the Tabernacle, the priesthood, the sacrifices, the means of worship, the mercy seat, the Day of Atonement, and on and on. Everywhere you look in Exodus, the story of redemption is told and dramatized. The Torah was given to reveal how God deals with transgressions among His people and how He intends to forgive them and restore the sinner to a place of fellowship.

Torah Reveals Redemption

What about Leviticus and Numbers? They are almost entirely given over to the issues of the priesthood, sacrifice, and daily matters of clean and unclean, pure and impure, and the means by which fellowship with God can be maintained in a fallen world. Once again, we understand Paul's point: Once the promise had been given, which would embrace a host of people within the covenant blessings, God "added" the Torah as His divine revelation of salvation through the sacrifice of an innocent substitute. For Paul, the Torah constantly and beautifully pointed toward Messiah and finds its goal in Him.[18]

And Deuteronomy? No other book in the Torah or the Prophets uses the Hebrew word *ahavah*, "love," more than Deuteronomy. This final book of Moses gathered the Torah covenant together as final words of warning, encouragement, instruction, and hope for the nation as she anticipated entering the

Promised Land. Quoted often in the Apostolic Scriptures, Deuteronomy continued to unfold God's plan of redemption and the central issues of repentance and faith within the scope of God's salvation.

Torah Teaches Forgiveness

If the promise of covenant blessings were to be viewed as a carefully crafted instrument, then the Torah is the instruction manual on how to use that instrument. When God chose Israel to be His covenant people, He gave them the Torah because He knew they were sinners and would need a way to return to Him after transgressing. Acted out in the daily life of the nation, the Torah taught the central message of forgiveness of sins through the substitutionary sacrifice of an innocent offering. Here, in the Torah, was the message of salvation by faith. So that is what Paul meant when he said that the Torah was given "because of transgressions."

This interpretation is bolstered by the additional lines in Galatians 3:19. "Why then the Torah? It was added because of transgressions, until the offspring should come to whom the promise had been made, and it was put in place through angels by an intermediary."[19]

First of all, in the statement "until the offspring should come to whom the promise had been made," the word *until* is often misunderstood. Many take this phrase of Paul to mean that the Torah existed until the coming of Messiah, and then ceased. But the word *until* in the Scriptures does not carry quite the same meaning as it does in English.

For example, note the well-known text of Psalm 110:

> The LORD says to my Lord: "Sit at My right hand until
> I make Your enemies a footstool for Your feet."

Surely the meaning here is not, "Sit at My right hand until I make your enemies a footstool for Your feet, and then You will no longer sit at My right hand." No. The meaning of *until* here,

If the promise of covenant blessings were to be viewed as a carefully crafted instrument, then the Torah is the instruction manual on how to use that instrument.

as often used in the Scriptures, means "with a view toward," or "as far as."[20] The Messiah sits at the right hand of the Almighty as the omnipotent warrior with a view to the subjugation of His enemies.

In similar manner, Paul's point is that the Torah was given to demonstrate God's method of dealing with transgressions with a view to the coming Seed in whom the promise would be realized. This is one reason it is important to have the clauses in this verse in the correct order. Unfortunately, some English translations (such as the NASB) transpose the order of the clauses to smooth out the translation, but in so doing, they unwittingly foil Paul's point. The Torah was given as a revelation of God's method of salvation—a revelation that is fully realized in Yeshua, the promised Seed.

Second, the final statement in Galatians 3:19, "It was put in place through angels by an intermediary," is likewise not negative but positive. The presence of angels at the giving of the Torah is well documented by the Apostolic Scriptures and is probably based upon Deuteronomy 33:2 (especially the LXX translation, which includes the word *angels*).[21] This Deuteronomy text was understood by the Jewish communities of Paul's day to picture the majestic entourage that accompanied the giving of the Torah on Mount Sinai.[22] And there is little doubt that Paul refers to Moses when he writes "by an intermediary." For any audience within the Jewish communities of the first century (and that included the congregation at Galatia), Moses was a majestic hero. Rather than putting the Torah in an inferior position, Paul's inclusion of angels and Moses at the giving of the Torah showed it to be of great value, granted to Israel with supreme pomp and circumstance. Indeed, in the ensuing context of Galatians 3, Paul shows that the Torah was God's ordained pedagogue to lead Israel to the Messiah. Far from being a trap to snare Israel in her sin, the Torah was God's holy assistant to guide His chosen ones in truth.

Conclusion

Perspective is all-important when we read the Scriptures. It's time for us to reconsider the "tools" in our workshops. Rather than presuming that the modern implements handed to us by teachers of the status quo are the best for getting the job done, we should recognize that the Scriptures themselves maintain a keener edge. Allowing the inspired Word of God to speak on its own terms will foster the recovery of the treasures those Scriptures hold. As we seek to foster communities that uphold the glory of Messiah Yeshua and that walk in His footsteps, we must show ourselves to be diligent craftsmen, "accurately handling the word of truth" (2 Timothy 2:15).

Summary

"The Law Was Given to Condemn"

"The law was given by God to teach mankind a hard lesson, as a kind of trap—a snare to entangle the sinner until he finally cries for help."

For the majority of contemporary Bible teachers, this is the starting point for interpreting what the Bible says about the Torah. Whenever the Torah is mentioned by the Apostles, it is interpreted with this negative perspective in mind. Granted, the Torah does have a condemning function. It reveals the righteous character of God against which all the actions of man are judged. And it rightly condemns sinners. That is one of its God-given functions. But should we presume that this is its only, or even its primary, function? Hardly! Torah was given to Israel to show how God deals with transgressions and particularly how He provides a way of forgiveness to those who are transgressors. While the common perspective of the Torah in Christendom is that it is a millstone around the neck of mankind, the Torah itself is primarily taken up with showing Israel the means by which she could have forgiveness and right standing with God.

"But Paul teaches that the law was given to deal with sin until Messiah came."

Paul's point is that the Torah was given to demonstrate God's method of dealing with transgressions with a view to the coming Seed in whom the promise would be realized. The Torah was given as a revelation of God's method of salvation—a revelation that is fully realized in Yeshua, the promised Seed. Indeed, in the context of Galatians 3, Paul shows that the Torah was God's ordained pedagogue to lead Israel to the Messiah. Far from being a trap to snare Israel in her sin, the Torah was God's holy assistant to guide His chosen ones in truth.

Study Questions

"The Law Was Given to Condemn"

1. Read and discuss Deuteronomy 30. What does this chapter tell us about God's commandments? Does this fit with the modern Christian's view of the Torah?
2. What has Judaism's view of the Torah been throughout history? Do we have the same view? Why or why not?
3. What was Paul's view of the Torah? Romans 3:31; 7:12, 14
4. What is Paul saying about salvation in verses 6-9? How does this relate to the story of Abraham in Genesis 22?
5. What is the context of Galatians 3? How does verse 17 effect our interpretation of verse 19?
6. Discuss the statement, "If the promise of covenant blessings were to be viewed as a carefully crafted instrument, then the Torah is the instruction manual on how to use that instrument." What light does this statement shed on Galatians 3?
7. What does the word *until* mean in Galatians 3:19? Does the interpretation "the Torah existed until the coming of Messiah and then ceased" fit within the context of Yeshua's teachings? (Matthew 5:17-19)
8. What did Paul's statement that "It was put in place through angels by an intermediary," mean to those who were listening? How did they view Moses and angels?

Rather than viewing the ingathering of the Gentiles as a separate and new work of God, the Apostles understood the salvation of the nations as the ongoing fulfillment of God's covenant promises to Israel. The Gentiles were being gathered into Israel, not forming a separate entity.

Is is Often Said

"The Church Replaced Israel"

How exactly should we define our modern word *church*? Is the *church* something new or ancient? Is it static or evolving? Is it eternal or temporal? These basic questions of ecclesiology (the doctrine of the church) have faced theologians since ancient times, and the answers supplied to these questions have shaped the various and diverse expressions of the Christian church throughout her history.

Two Theological Systems

Perhaps one question regarding the identification of the church stands above the others: What is the relationship of the church to Israel? Two general answers have been given. In the first one the church replaces Israel, who as a nation ceases to be, and a spiritual entity, "the church," becomes God's 'new Israel.' In the second one the church is something new, and it comprises God's work primarily among the nations until He once again turns His attention to the nation of Israel in the last days.

Supersessionism

In the first case, which we call "replacement theology" or "supersessionism," Israel (redefined as the church) is eternal. There are no gaps or breaks. The ancient nation of Israel gives way to the spiritual family of God called "the church." From the vantage point of those who hold this theology, God has not abandoned Israel—He has replaced unbelieving Israel with the "new Israel," the church. This theology is usually the stance of those who call themselves covenant theologians, and often amillennialism is the natural conclusion of covenant theology. Amillennialism, as the name implies, sees no thousand-year reign of the Messiah upon the earth, ruling over a restored Israel. Since Israel has been replaced, the rule and reign of Messiah over Israel is a present reality (albeit spiritual and non-physical). Physical Israel is out of the picture.

Likewise, in the second theological option, God has not abandoned Israel. He has simply held her in suspension while He turns His attention to the church. Once He has completed His purposes in the church and taken her out of the world, He will once again turn His efforts toward national Israel and fulfill His covenant promises to her. This viewpoint is that of dispensational theology and most often some form of premillennialism is its natural adjunct. As the name implies, premillennialism sees the second coming of Messiah occurring before His thousand-year reign upon the earth.

Both covenant theology and dispensationalism are methods of interpreting the Bible (each with its own hermeneutic). Covenant theology, generally claiming that the church has replaced Israel, must adopt some kind of allegorical interpretation, for it is driven by the need to find a deeper or fuller sense (*sensus plenior*) in the Scriptures, since literal Israel must ultimately give way to spiritual Israel. The literal meaning of the inspired words is abandoned for a "deeper" and more "mystical" understanding.

Thus, the physical gives way to the non-physical (usually called spiritual). For example, the Sabbath as a memorial of creation gives way to the Sabbath as a memorial to redemption.[23] For the covenant theologian, the pattern is clear: Sabbath of the old Israel gives way to Sunday (the day of resurrection=redemption) for the new Israel. Circumcision of the old Israel gives way to baptism of the new Israel. (Thus infants are baptized in the same way that infants were circumcised.) Whereas circumcision was the means of entering the covenant for old Israel, baptism becomes the means of covenant entrance for the new Israel. Festivals or appointed times give way to new celebrations of the Messiah (Christmas and Easter). In short, all of the promises made to old Israel are fulfilled spiritually in the new Israel. And of course, the new Israel is the church.

Dispensationalism

Dispensationalism reacted against the deeply entrenched, allegorical hermeneutics of covenant theology. Seeing the slippery slope of allegorical interpretation, dispensationalism returned (at least in theory) to a grammatical, historical interpretation of the Bible. The problem, of course, came with how the church related to Israel. Developing a schema of dispensations (periods of time) in which God's requirements for obedience differed from one era to the next, dispensationalism taught the idea of the "suspension of prophecy." God's covenant promises to Israel were suspended because of her disobedience, but not abandoned. While Israel's "prophetic clock" was stopped, God turned His attention to a new entity, the church, and the ingathering of the Gentiles. Once He has completed His work in the church, Israel's clock will be restarted, and she will be brought to obedience and faith. In this way, the covenant promises made to Israel will be fulfilled in the millennium and ultimately in the world to come.

For the dispensationalist, the problem of hermeneutics was not to find the deeper or fuller sense, but to distinguish between those Scriptures that directly applied to Israel and those that applied to the church. Most obvious in this regard was the Law, or the Torah. This belonged to Israel, not to the church, and to the former dispensations, not the current church age. In much the same way, though the *Tanakh* contained many principles and teachings for the church, it, too, was viewed as having its primary application to Israel. Conversely, the Apostolic Scriptures (New Testament) embodied the Scriptures for the church.

Thus, the two systems of theology are contrasted not only in how each viewed Israel, but also in how each dealt with continuity or discontinuity. Covenant theology seeks to stress continuity: Israel is God's people throughout all time. "Old Israel" is replaced by "new Israel," and what was given to old Israel is more fully given to new Israel. Dispensationalism, on the other hand, emphasizes discontinuity: Israel and the church are entirely distinct, with distinct purposes, covenants, and destinies.

Obviously, this is an oversimplified description of covenant theology and dispensationalism. Some in both camps would take exception to the pigeon holes I've described. Still, in the broad scope of things, the characterizations I've offered fit the basic tenets of these two systems of theology and hermeneutics. Moreover, these two systems have, by and large, been the warp and woof of Christian theology for centuries, so much so that many aspects of these theologies are taken for granted by their respective groups as "just the way things are." Indeed, these two systems have worked for those who see themselves as either replacing Israel or as entirely distinct from Israel.

The Prophets' Theology

But what do the Scriptures say? How do the prophets describe the ingathering of God's elect from the nations and their relationship to Israel? And what is the view of Yeshua and His Apostles?

First, it should be obvious to us that the covenant God made with Abraham was passed to his descendants as well. Thus, the covenant is renewed to Isaac and Jacob, and affirmed as the reason for God's redemption of Israel in the exodus. In Exodus 2:24 we read, "So God heard their groaning; and God remembered His covenant with Abraham, Isaac, and Jacob." It was the

The congregation of Israel was called an *ekklesia* throughout the Septuagint. And throughout the Apostolic era, the *ekklesia* is considered a grouping within Israel.

Abrahamic covenant that formed the basis for the exodus of the nation of Israel from Egypt—several hundred years later.

Likewise, the Sinai covenant was made with the nation as a whole. Moreover, the New Covenant prophesied by Jeremiah (31:31–34) is on a national scale: "Behold, days are coming," declares the LORD, "when I will make a new covenant with the house of Israel and with the house of Judah."

The point I am making is that the covenants that promised redemptive blessing were made with one nation and one nation alone: the nation of Israel. Thus Amos writes (3:2), "You only have I chosen (literally, "known") among all the families of the earth." As far as the prophets are concerned, God's covenant blessings are focused upon one people only: Israel.

However, the prophets also recognized that from the beginning God blessed individuals from "the nations"—those outside of Israel who had no traceable lineage to Jacob. But whenever God's chosen of the nations come into the covenant, they do so by joining Israel. The covenant blessings do not flow outside of Israel to the nations. Rather, the chosen ones of the nations come into Israel, where they enjoy the salvation that God secures for His people.

This is the picture represented by Isaiah who likewise sees the millennial Temple as the house of prayer for all the peoples.[24] Zechariah prophesied about Gentiles taking hold of the hem of the Jew in order to learn about God.[25] Everywhere in the Prophets, the blessing of salvation upon the Gentiles comes only as they come into Israel. There is not even a hint among the prophetic literature that the chosen Gentiles would be formed into a separate people and blessed with God's presence apart from Israel.

Thus, the prophets know nothing of a "church age" in which the covenant promises to Israel are suspended, and God turns His attention to the Gentiles apart from Israel (as dispensationalism teaches). So obvious was this to the early framers of dispensationalism that they considered the church age a parenthesis in the flow of prophetic history about which the prophets knew nothing.

Nor do the prophets teach that Israel would be lost and replaced by the chosen of the nations (as covenant theology teaches). For the prophets, the same nation that was exiled and punished for her sins would be the nation that returns to the Land by the divine hand of the Almighty.[26] What is more, the returned captives of Israel will be blessed with a new covenant that promises salvation through the outpouring of the Spirit and a genuine faith in God's Messiah, for their sins will be forgiven and their transgressions no longer remembered.[27]

Yeshua taught the same message. While His primary focus was upon the "lost sheep of Israel," He nonetheless spoke of "other sheep," not of "this fold," which would also join the flock under His care.[28] Moreover, having seen the faith of the centurion, the Master commented, "Many will come from east and west and recline at the table with Abraham, Isaac and Jacob in the kingdom of heaven" (Matthew 8:11). Yeshua's vision of the ingathering of the Gentiles was not to their own table or their own separate identity, but as those who were gathered to Israel, to become part of God's covenant people.

The Apostles' Theology

Paul's message was the same. In the powerful metaphor of the olive tree in Romans 11, he gives a graphic illustration of how God engrafts the believing Gentiles into the covenant people of Israel, supported and nourished by the covenant promises of the root. He teaches in Ephesians 2 that those who were far off (the Gentiles) are brought near, and with Israel's Messiah they overcome their detachment from the "commonwealth of Israel." For Paul, to be "in Messiah" is to be in Israel. Not some ethereal, philosophical, or theological "Israel," but Israel as the physical, living, and abiding people of God. From Paul's perspective, the remnant is comprised of Jew and non-Jew who have believed in Yeshua, and the remnant throughout every generation participates in the covenant blessings promised to the fathers. This is not to deny that the physical offspring of Jacob also participate in the temporal blessings of the covenant. Yet apart from genuine faith in Yeshua, even the physical descendants will eventually be cut off from the covenant blessings if they persist in their unbelief. Only in the final *eschaton*[29] is all Israel saved when God's faithfulness to Israel is demonstrated by His completion of the New Covenant promises.[30]

Some might argue that the church was nonexistent before the coming of the Messiah. But such a view is based upon a reading of the English translations only. If we were to look for the word *ekklesia* (the Greek word translated "church" in the Apostolic Scriptures), we would find it throughout the Greek translation of the *Tanakh*. No one in the time of Yeshua or the Apostolic era would have considered the *ekklesia* to denote a new concept. The congregation of Israel was called an *ekklesia* throughout the Septuagint. And throughout the Apostolic era, the *ekklesia* is considered a grouping within Israel, both by those who were followers of Yeshua and by those who were not. Even the Roman government considered the people of "The Way" to be one of the sects of Judaism, part of the congregation (*ekklesia*) of Israel. The split that occurred in the second and third centuries between the emerging Christian church and the extant Judaisms finds no basis in the Apostolic Scriptures.

Yet this eventual split between the Christian church and the synagogue forged a meaning for the English word *church* in the later centuries. In our times the word *church* is used to denote a religion entirely separate from the religion of the synagogue and, by extension, separate from Israel. When we read the Apostolic Scriptures with this later meaning in mind, we derive the erroneous teaching that the church is something new—a new people of God. Yet for the writers of Scripture, the word *ekklesia* did not denote a group separate from Israel, but a community within Israel who constituted the faithful remnant. For them, the ingathering of the Gentiles to faith in the God of Israel through His Messiah, Yeshua, was a portent of God's final victory in saving all of Israel. Rather than viewing the ingathering of the Gentiles as a separate and new work of God, the Apostles understood the salvation of the nations as the ongoing fulfillment of God's covenant promises to Israel. The Gentiles were being gathered into Israel, not forming a separate entity.

A New Picture Emerges

This theological picture is different from either covenant or dispensational theologies. Rather than replacing Israel, or setting Israel aside temporarily, this approach sees the ingathering of the Gentiles as expanding Israel. To illustrate, let's use Paul's olive tree metaphor as depicting the covenant people of God. Covenant theology would have the tree cut down and another planted in its place. Dispensational theology would leave the olive tree standing, but would plant a second tree alongside it. As we examine the text, however, we see that Paul's picture is of wild branches (believing Gentiles) being grafted into the original olive tree. Not replacement and not something new and separate, but seeing the remnant within Israel as a foreshadowing of the final salvation of the *eschaton*, when all Israel will be saved.

This approach has wide ramifications for the current Torah movement. First, there is a vast difference between "the Jewish roots of our Christian faith" and being grafted into Israel. The Jewish roots movement enjoys the story of the past without necessarily seeing how this story impacts the present and the future. How many times have we heard wonderful teachings about the Sabbath, the festivals, or the value of the *mitzvot,* (commandments) only to hear at the end of the teaching that all of these things have now passed away? In the Jewish Roots movement, it seems that too often the root is severed from the reality of the fruit we are supposed to bring forth.

Second, a realization of actually being brought into the covenant people of God makes a significant difference on the issue of our identity. We have come to realize that God does not have two peoples, each with their own calling and mission. We do not see the church as the place for believing Gentiles, and Messianic congregations as the place for believing Jews. What we long to see is all of God's people embracing the covenant of salvation and redemption that He promised to His chosen ones, a covenant that identifies our current walk in sanctification, as well as our hope for the world to come. This means that in our efforts to spread the Good News, we are not attempting to bring Israel into the church, but we are hopeful that through the Gospel, many Gentiles will be grafted into Israel, and that the chosen remnant of the Jews will embrace Yeshua as Messiah.

Finally, by understanding our identity within Israel, we take the Torah seriously, not as a means to some other end, but as the normal manner of life for the covenant people of God. We do not see the *Tanakh* as the foreword to the real important message of the Apostles, nor as though we are reading someone else's mail. The Torah becomes our *ketubah* (marriage contract) not someone else's. We see ourselves under the marriage *chuppah,* not in the audience. We find our belonging by participation in the covenant, not as bystanders observing someone else's wedding day. This changes the way we look at the Torah, and it changes our motivations for observing its precepts. We have come into the family of God; therefore, the life prescribed for His family is our life, our calling, our destiny.

Summary

"The Church Replaced Israel"

"The church replaced Israel, who as a nation ceased to be, and the spiritual entity, the church, became God's 'new Israel.'"

The prophets do not teach that Israel would be lost and replaced by the chosen of the nations (as covenant theology teaches). For the prophets, the same nation that was exiled and punished for her sins would be the nation that returns to the Land by the divine hand of the Almighty. What is more, the returned captives of Israel will be blessed with a new covenant that promises salvation through the outpouring of the Spirit and a genuine faith in God's Messiah, for their sins will be forgiven and their transgressions no longer remembered.

"God has discontinued His attention on Israel to focus on the church. In the last days, God will again focus His attention on the nation of Israel."

To illustrate, let's use Paul's olive tree metaphor as depicting the covenant people of God. Dispensational theology would leave the olive tree standing, but would plant a second tree alongside it. As we examine the text, however, we see that Paul's picture is of wild branches (believing Gentiles) being grafted into the original olive tree. Not replacement and not something new and separate, but seeing the remnant within Israel as a foreshadowing of the final salvation of the *eschaton*, when all Israel will be saved. Rather than viewing the ingathering of the Gentiles as a separate and new work of God, the Apostles understood the salvation of the nations as the ongoing fulfillment of God's covenant promises to Israel. The Gentiles were being gathered into Israel, not forming a separate entity.

"The church is something new. It was nonexistent before the coming of the Messiah."

Such a view is based upon a reading of the English translations of scripture only. If we were to look for the word *ekklesia* (the Greek word translated "church" in the Apostolic Scriptures), we would find it throughout the Greek translation of the *Tanakh*. No one in the time of Yeshua or the Apostolic era would have considered the *ekklesia* to denote a new concept. The congregation of Israel was called an *ekklesia* throughout the Septuagint. And throughout the Apostolic era, the *ekklesia* is considered a grouping within Israel, both by those who were followers of Yeshua and by those who were not. In our times the word *church* is used to denote a religion entirely separate from the religion of the synagogue and, by extension, separate from Israel. When we read the Apostolic Scriptures with this later meaning in mind, we derive the erroneous teaching that the church is something new—a new people of God.

Study Questions

"The Church Replaced Israel"

1. Discuss supersessionism and dispensationalism. What are the foundational beliefs of these two theologies?
2. How do these two theological views fit with the teachings of the prophets? (Jeremiah 23:5–8; 31:31–34; Amos 3:2; Isaiah 40:2; 44:3; 56:3–5; 56:7; Zechariah 8:23; 9:12; 12:10)

3. How do these two theological views fit with the teachings of Yeshua? (John 10:16; Matthew 8:11; 10:6; 15:24)

4. And how do they fit with the teachings of Paul the Apostle? (Romans 11; Ephesians 2)

5. What is the Greek word for *church*? Who does it describe in the Greek Septuagint? Based on this information, is the *church* a new concept?

The picture given in the Prophets
is Jew and Gentile together in one
place, worshipping in one way,
"equal and together," communing
in a unified covenant identity.
Not two peoples, but one and
not two Torahs, but one.

Is is Often Said

"The Torah is Only for Jews"

A wonderful thing is happening in our times: There is a renewed awakening to the beauty of the Torah (God's teaching found in the first five books of the Bible). Many are realizing that it is the foundation of God's gracious covenant relationship with those He has called to be His people. Decades of anti-Torah biases are being set aside as individuals return to the study of the Scriptures, and find in them God's enduring message of grace, righteousness, and promise.

Such a revival, however, is not without its opponents. As in the early decades of the emerging Christian church which saw her leaders speaking against the Torah, so we regularly hear those who continue to teach that the Torah was abolished by the coming of Yeshua. They say that His death and resurrection has ushered in a "new way," a salvation that is in every way superior to what the Torah teaches. As a result, charges of "legalism" and "going back under the Law" are commonly lodged against those of us who are teaching the enduring viability of the Torah in the lives of believers.

I want to deal with a belief not only held by some in mainline Christian theologies, but also heard from teachers within Messianic Judaism. This is the view that the Torah is the special possession of the Jewish people and that many of its stipulations are therefore directed toward Jews, not Gentiles. Those who take this position believe that while the moral aspects of the Torah are universal for all of God's children, the various stipulations of the Torah that are particularly covenantal are for the Jewish people only, given to them as distinct marks of their unique position in the covenant made with Israel. These could include such things as the Sabbath, festivals, kosher laws, wearing of *tzitzit* (tassels, cf. Numbers 15:37ff) and generally all the things in the Torah that mark Israel as distinct from the nations. In some cases, non-Jews who wish to obey these aspects of Torah are criticized as taking on themselves those things that belong uniquely to the Jewish people. Furthermore, the teaching that the whole Torah is the possession and responsibility of all of God's children is labeled as theological error and therefore dangerous for the body of Messiah, because when non-Jews live out Torah, the lines of distinction between Jew and non-Jew are blurred.

"Torah is Only for Jews"—The Current Controversy

The current belief that the "Gentile Christian church" is the assembly of the faithful from the nations, and that Messianic Judaism is the proper place for believing Jews is prevalent among many Messianic Jewish congregations and even some Christian churches. This theology is left with no alternative but to affirm that the Torah and the "rich tradition" it possesses is not for all believers. Significant parts of it are only for the Jews. Where does this leave the non-Jewish member of the Messianic congregation? Or the Jewish member of the Gentile church?

What does the Torah teach about non-Jews within the covenant? Is there any indication that the Torah is for some and not for others? And what did the Apostles teach? How did they handle these same issues as Gentiles flooded into the community of believers called "The Way"?

The Words *Ger* and *Proselyte*

The primary word used throughout the *Tanakh* for the non-Jew who has joined himself to Israel is the word *ger*, derived from the verb *gur*, meaning "wandering" or "sojourning." A *ger* is one who, because of war, famine, or other factors, has left his village or tribe and sought refuge in another place in which his rights of land ownership and normal citizenship have been curtailed.[31]

The word *ger* is sometimes linked with other words, acting as modifiers or descriptors. A study of the word in the *Tanakh* shows, however, that there are no clear classifications of the *ger* based upon the various terms used. In each case, the place of the *ger* within the larger community of Israel must be discerned by the surrounding context. Furthermore, it is clear that the word *ger* had primarily a sociological meaning, not a religious one. It can describe a foreigner who has simply come within the community of Israel as well as a foreigner who worships the one true God of Abraham, Isaac, and Jacob. When the context makes it clear that the *ger* has indeed attached himself to the God of Israel, it is often plainly stated that the *ger* and the native born have the same privileges and responsibilities as covenant members.[32]

While the word *ger* always bears a sociological meaning in the *Tanakh*, there came a time when the sages began to understand it in a religious sense. As Israel was exiled and ruled by foreign powers, Jewish identity was constantly challenged. More and more, covenant membership was tied to Jewish ethnicity as the nation struggled for survival. And as covenant membership became tied to ethnic status, the position of the non-Jew within Israel also changed. If the non-Jew wanted full covenant membership, he would have to cut all ties to his Gentile past and "become a Jew." "Becoming a Jew" meant that the sociological category of "native born" had now been combined with a religious category of "covenant member." In this view, the native born were covenant members by birth (since covenant membership was based upon ethnicity), but the "sojourner" would have to change ethnic status through a "ritual of conversion." Central to this man-made ritual was circumcision, the sign of the covenant.

Thus, with this new perspective, the sages began to reinterpret the term *ger* as they found it in the *Tanakh*. In places where it seemed that the *ger* was functioning as a covenant member, they gave it the meaning "convert" or "proselyte." In other places the word retained its original meaning of "foreigner" or "alien."

This shift may also be noted in the LXX. The word *proselutos* ("proselyte") is the normal term used to translate *ger*. However, in contexts where *ger* does not fit the rabbinic understanding of "convert," the LXX sometimes substitutes other words. It would appear that their choice of words may have been influenced by the rabbinic theology of their day.

This also changed the way texts were interpreted by the sages. The new theology of covenant membership based upon ethnic status was read back into the Torah. That this is still the case today is seen, for instance, in the translation of *ger* in the Stone Chumash. Wherever a *ger* is assigned Torah privileges and responsibilities, the term is translated as "proselyte" or "convert." But where the meaning "proselyte" or "convert" is not appropriate, the word *alien* or equivalent is used. Note, for example, the Stone translation of Leviticus 19:34:

> The proselyte (*ger*) who dwells with you shall be like a native among you, and you shall love him like yourself, for you were aliens (*gerim*) in the land of Egypt—I am HASHEM your God.[33]

It would not make sense to be consistent and translate "for you were proselytes in the land of Egypt." Here, the word *ger* clearly means "sojourner" in both cases, but the prevailing theology of the rabbis affected their translation.

No one confined to the biblical record itself would come up with the idea that there should be two separate expressions of the body of Messiah, the "Gentile Christian church" and "Messianic Judaism."

This shift in theology, which required that *ger* sometimes be interpreted as a "convert," also necessitated new rabbinic terms to differentiate between the non-Jew and the "convert." Thus, the rabbis reinterpreted the common Torah designation *ger toshav*, "resident alien," as a non-convert; i.e., a Gentile. They in turn developed a new term, *ger tzadik*, to designate "a righteous *ger*," a Gentile who had converted. The term *ger tzadik*, of course, is not found in the *Tanakh*.[34] But it is significant that the rabbis chose the word *tzadik*, "righteous," to describe the convert. The emerging rabbinic theology had determined that only Israel was righteous; therefore, to credit righteousness to a non-Jew was only possible if he "became a Jew" through the man-made ritual.[35]

The ritual of conversion consisted of four things, though as the theology of conversion was being hammered out, there were debates on the necessity of all four. The rabbis required the convert to (1) submit to the Torah (both written and oral), (2) receive circumcision, (3) undergo a *mikveh* (ritual bath), and (4) offer a sacrifice. After the destruction of the Temple, payment of money was substituted for the sacrifice.

However, such a ceremony or "ritual of conversion" is not found in the Bible. Throughout the Scriptures, covenant membership was not based upon one's bloodline, but upon one's faith in the God of Abraham, Isaac, and Jacob, a faith evidenced by a willingness to live out the Torah He had given His covenant people. What is more, covenant membership did not change one's ethnicity. From the beginning God intended that "all the nations of the earth" would be blessed in Abraham. They would be blessed, not by becoming Jews or changing their ethnicity (something that is, of course, impossible), but by becoming full covenant members as those who were not physically descended from Jacob but who had been equally chosen by God to be part of His covenant people.

It seems clear that the current issues are fueled by the influence of the rabbinic perspective. No one confined to the biblical record itself would come up with the idea that there should be two separate expressions of the body of Messiah, the "Gentile Christian church" and "Messianic Judaism." Nor could anyone derive from the Bible a "ritual of conversion" that changed the ethnic status of a Gentile into that of a Jew. The very fact that such a proposal could find acceptance in our day stems back to the rabbinic perspective and the rabbinic Judaism that emerged from it. It cannot be sustained from the Scriptures.

The Covenant People

The name "Israel" is first encountered as the new name given to Jacob at the renewal of the Abrahamic covenant (Genesis 32:28). Its meaning is not certain, though traditionally it has been understood to mean "He contends with God."[36] The name "Israel" is first used in a national sense in Exodus 4:22, when God declares, "Israel is ... My firstborn." Most often, however, the common designation for the twelve tribes of Israel is "children of Israel" (*b'nei Israel*).[37] This phrase, using the word *son* (*bein*) in the sense of "child," refers to both male and female who make up the nation of Israel.[38] But foreigners were also part of the people called the "children of Israel." The Exodus narrative is clear that a "mixed multitude" went up from Egypt (Exodus 12:38), a designation that includes both native born and foreigner together.

Yet the text always refers to Israel as the people God redeemed:

> And on that same day the LORD brought the sons of Israel out of the land of Egypt by their hosts. (Exodus 12:51)

So when the record indicates that God redeemed the sons of Israel, it must mean that those non-Jews who had attached themselves to Israel were considered a bona fide part of God's people. As far as the Exodus narrative is concerned, Israel, whom God redeemed from Egypt, was comprised of both native born and "sojourners" or "foreigners."

It is this same mixed multitude that stood at the foot of Mount Sinai and accepted the covenant of the Torah. According to Exodus 19, the people redeemed from Egypt by God's power are those who arrived at Sinai. And when the covenant terms were announced to the people, the text states: "All the people answered together and said, 'All that the LORD has spoken we will do!'" (Exodus 19:8). The native born together with the foreigner constituted the covenant people who received the Torah at Sinai.

Moreover, the fact that the biblical text continues to instruct the nation of Israel to treat the foreigner with respect and justice proves that the *ger* retained the status of foreigner even while functioning as a full covenant member.[39]

That the *ger* is considered a covenant member, receiving both the privileges and responsibilities of the covenant, is clear from the activities in which he engages and the covenant consequences assigned to him. He participates in the yearly festivals and is required to observe the statutes of the Torah (Deuteronomy 31:12).[40] The *ger* brings sacrifices to the Lord,[41] is not allowed to eat blood (Leviticus 17:11–13), becomes unclean when eating meat from animals dead or torn (Leviticus 17:15), participates in the ritual of the ashes of the red heifer (Numbers 19:10), receives the death penalty for idolatry or cursing God (Leviticus 20:2; 24:16), participates in corporate forgiveness (Numbers 15:26), and may be cut off from the community for defiance against God (Numbers 19:10), which presupposes that he is a full-fledged member of the community.

The Abrahamic and Mosaic Covenants

Abrahamic	Mosaic
Special relationship: Genesis 17:7	**Treasured people**: Exodus 19:5
Gift of the land: Genesis 15:18-19	**Gift of the land**: Exodus 23:20-33
Increase in number: Genesis 17:6	**Increase in number**: Leviticus 26:9
Confirm covenant to next generation: Genesis 17:7	**Confirm covenant to next generation**: Leviticus 26:9
Be your God/You shall be My people: Genesis 17:7	**Be your God/You shall be My people**: Leviticus 26:12
General blessing: Genesis 12:2; 26:24	**General blessing**: Deuteronomy 11:26f
Nations blessed: Genesis 12:3; 28:14, et al	**Nations come to the light of the Torah**: Deut 32:43; 33:19; Isaiah 2:3; 51:4

A study of the covenants God made with Abraham and his offspring tell the same story. Did not God promise blessing upon the nations as part of the covenant?[42] What is more, the subsequent Sinai covenant is presented, not as a competing covenant, but as an expression of God's continuing faithfulness to the covenant He made with Abraham. In fact, in the unfolding of the covenant narratives, the Sinai covenant is clearly given as the means by which the blessings of the Abrahamic covenant would be realized. We see this by the fact that the promises of the Abrahamic covenant, given unconditionally (unilateral), are repeated in the Mosaic covenant as contingent upon obedience (bilateral).[43]

The two covenants, then, are not separate and distinct, but are woven together in the flow of redemptive history. The covenant given to Abraham, which promised blessing, land, an enduring covenant relationship between the offspring of Abraham and God, and covenant blessing for all the nations, is reaffirmed in the Mosaic covenant and the giving of the Torah. It is not as though God has gone back on His word, at first promising unconditional blessing to Abraham, and then changing His covenant to be conditional at Sinai. Far from it! God, in choosing Abraham and his offspring, was forming a people who would be characterized by His own holiness. The covenant of Abraham came not only with blessing, but also with provision to attain that blessing through obedience.

> The LORD said, "Shall I hide from Abraham what I am about to do, since Abraham will surely become a great and mighty nation, and in him all the nations of the earth will be blessed? For I have chosen him, so that he may command his children and his household after him to keep the way of the LORD by doing righteousness and justice, so that the LORD may bring upon Abraham what He has spoken about him." (Genesis 18:17–19).

Thus, the Mosaic covenant, the Torah, is given to bring about that holiness which would, in turn, procure the promised covenant blessings. To the extent that the Abrahamic covenant both envisioned and incorporated the nations, so the Mosaic covenant, the Torah, is given to all covenant members as the divine revelation of God's holiness, written upon the heart of every covenant member, in order to bring about God's blessings in their lives and in the life of the covenant nation.

In this way, the two covenants function as two sides of the same coin. Like justification and sanctification as described in the Scriptures, both of which are necessary for the salvation of the sinner, so the Abrahamic covenant and the Mosaic covenant are bound together in God's salvific plan. The Abrahamic covenant is presented as unilateral (God initiating and promising) just as justification is God's sole work. Likewise, the Mosaic covenant is presented as bilateral (God and Israel working together) just as sanctification is presented in the Bible as the cooperation between the redeemed soul and the Almighty. In this same manner, Paul presents the gospel as enveloped within the Abrahamic promise, connected to the Mosaic covenant as the pedagogue to lead to the Promised One (Galatians 3).

No one would deny that the Gentiles are envisioned in the Abrahamic covenant ("In you all the nations of the earth shall be blessed"). But if the Abrahamic covenant includes the Gentiles, then so does the Mosaic covenant, for the Mosaic covenant is given as the means of fulfilling the covenant promises made to Abraham. The two covenants are bound together—they cannot be separated. To say that the Gentiles are blessed in the Abrahamic covenant but have no part in the Mosaic covenant would be like saying a person could be justified without becoming sanctified. Such a scenario finds no place in the biblical record.

To Draw Near

From the earliest times, the glory of the Torah given to Israel attracted foreign peoples to worship the God of Abraham, Isaac, and Jacob. This is in accordance with what God promised in Deuteronomy 4:5–8. This motif of the foreigner coming to worship the God of Israel is incorporated into Solomon's dedicatory prayer in 1 Kings 8:41–43. Other terminology is found in the *Tanakh* that indicates the attachment of non-Israelites to the covenant nation. Ruth is said to have sought refuge by coming under the "wings" of the Almighty, a metaphor the psalmist also uses of finding companionship with God in His "tent."[44] Ruth's famous confession includes both a connection to the people and to the God of Israel, "Your people shall be my people, and your God, my God" (Ruth 1:16)

The promise made to the fathers was being realized in the salvation of the Gentiles. The future had invaded the present.

But how should we understand the Torah commandment prohibiting the Ammonites or Moabites from entering the assembly of Israel?[45] Ruth was a Moabitess. The only conclusion possible is that Ruth lost the penalty attributed to a Moabite (even though she is consistently remembered as such) when, through her own confession, she joined the people of Israel. Yet any ritual of conversion is entirely lacking in the biblical narrative. She became a full-fledged covenant member through her confession of belief in God and her willingness to become attached to the people of Israel through her marriage to Boaz.

A common expression in the Torah is "the alien (*ger*) who is "in your midst (*b'kerev*).[46] The word *kerev* is connect to the verb *karav*, "to draw near." The idea of "drawing near" is reflected in the words of Paul in Ephesians 2, where the Gentile is said to have been "far off" but has been "brought near" through faith in Yeshua.[47] For Paul, the negative condition of the Gentiles, that they were separate from the covenants of (the) promise, is overcome by being brought near through the blood of Messiah.

To "draw near" (*karav*) is connected with the Tabernacle or Temple ceremony and with the sacrifices. Indeed, to "offer" a sacrifice is denoted by the term "bring near," and especially "to bring near to the Lord."[48] Furthermore, in reference to the priests, to "draw near to God," means to offer sacrifices—to be in communion with God.[49] As the priests represented the people before the altar, in their "drawing near to God," they brought the covenant people into communion with God. Thus, "drawing near to God" has clear covenant ramifications.

Moreover, for Paul, this covenant relationship that the Gentiles now possess is nothing less than being included in the "commonwealth of Israel" from which they were formerly far off. Paul's emphasis upon the fact that the "circumcision" (those who based their covenant status upon being Jewish) called the Gentiles the "uncircumcision" (not Jewish) shows that in his day the prevailing view of the Jewish community was that "drawing near" was possible only for Jews. This left only one alternative for Gentiles as far as the rabbis were concerned: They would have to become Jewish (proselytes) in order to enter the covenant. But Paul's theology could not sustain such a position, because the Scriptures speak differently.

In the context of Ephesians 3, Paul makes it clear that the Gentiles do not form a separate entity, nor do they participate in a covenant different from the Jews, but the Gentiles are fellow heirs and fellow members of the body, and fellow partakers of the promise in Messiah Yeshua through the gospel.[50]

When Paul uses the metaphoric word *body*, he is not referring to some theological category that exists only in a creed. He is rather describing the physical community of believers existing in a given place and time. They meet with one another, bear one another's burdens, exhort and encourage one another, and serve one another through the spiritual enabling they have received.

The Gospel, as far as Paul was concerned, is grounded in the Abrahamic promise that all of the nations would be blessed through his seed.[51] This blessing accords with the eschatological promise that the nations would be instructed in the Torah; not in their separate locations, but as they came up to Zion and fulfilled Isaiah's prophecy that the Temple would be called the "house of prayer for all the peoples."[52] For Paul, the "body of Messiah" is the current representation of the final and ultimate victory of the kingdom when Messiah will reign upon the earth.

Consider Paul's rebuke of Peter in Galatians 2. He confronted him over issues of "table fellowship," that is, the *halachah*[53] about who could eat with whom, particularly the issue of Jews and non-Jews eating together. To Paul, Peter's position was wrong and something that could not stand in the face of the Gospel. Peter, at one point, had eaten with the believing Gentiles, but when in the presence of the Jewish brethren who were following a different *halachah*, he withdrew. Why would this be so significant in Paul's mind? Because he recognized that table fellowship expressed a central covenant issue. Far from thinking that the Jews could have one table and the Gentiles another, Paul saw in the words of the *Tanakh* a single table at which all of God's chosen people sit and fellowship. Eating together at a common table was evidence of their mutual covenant membership and envisioned the fulfillment of Yeshua's prophecy that many would come from east and west to sit at the table with Abraham, Isaac, and Jacob.[54]

Indeed, the vision of the prophets is that the nations would come to Jerusalem to celebrate the feast of Sukkot, the *mo'ed* (appointed time) that consummates the festival cycle (Zechariah 14:16ff). They would worship the God of Israel, sitting together in the *sukkah*. This is not some perfunctory duty, for the nations have come to seek Israel's covenant God, grasping the hem of a Jewish person as an entreaty to learn of Israel's God and enter the covenant.[55] The point of this prophecy is that the Gentiles should "go with" the Jew to learn and to worship, not find their own separate worship and identity. Isaiah also speaks of the foreigner who attaches himself to the Lord and of foreigners who attached themselves to Jacob.[56]

In these prophets, the picture is not "equal but separate," as though there were two groups that have equal covenant status but congregate in their own respective places. Rather it is Jew and Gentile together in one place, worshipping in one way, "equal and together," communing in a unified covenant identity. Not two peoples, but one; not two Torahs, but one; not two sets of *halachot*, but one. Thus, the covenant expressions of the Torah, ascribing the same Torah to both native born and foreigner, are realized in the body of Messiah as a foreshadowing of the ultimate reign of Messiah in the millennial kingdom and the world to come.[57] In Paul's day, the beginning of this "one people, one covenant, one Torah," was evident. The promise made to the fathers was being realized in the salvation of the Gentiles.[58] The future had invaded the present.

Adoption

The metaphor of adoption is used in Scripture to picture how God brings people into His family. Adoption was common in the ancient Semitic world. Records show that adoption was used to give a person legal status and privilege. For that reason, wives were adopted, as were brothers and sisters, slaves, as well as orphans. In many cases, adoption was a legal means of assuring inheritance would pass to the adopted individual.[59]

God chose Abraham for the purpose of covenant; that is, to give him legal status in His world.[60] The giving of land is an integral part of the covenant (Genesis 15) and shows that God chose Abraham to give him legal ownership of territory which, though occupied by other peoples, was God's possession to give to His chosen people. "Choosing" may well be adoption language.

God also chose the offspring of Jacob:

> For you are a holy people to the LORD your God; the LORD your God has chosen you to be a people for His own possession out of all the peoples who are on the face of the earth. (Deuteronomy 7:6)

We see the adoption procedure when Jacob blesses Ephraim and Manasseh. Placing them between (or upon) his knees was symbolic of adoption, since the phrase "to bear on my knees" was legal language for an heir.[61] Thus, Ephraim and Manasseh became Joseph's brothers and shared in the inheritance equally with the others. After the adoption ceremony in which Jacob placed his hands upon Joseph's sons and pronounced a blessing over them, legally they were no longer Joseph's sons but his brothers. They entered into the inheritance of Jacob as equals with Joseph and the rest of Jacob's sons.

In fact, Ezekiel portrays the Exodus itself as an act of adoption, for he pictures Israel as an aborted baby, the offspring of an Amorite father and a Hittite mother. Viewing the baby in its blood, the Almighty has compassion on it, chooses it for Himself, and adopts it as His own child.[62] Despite the fact that Israel is described as the offspring of the Amorites and the Hittites, the most pagan of nations in Israel's history, Israel is chosen to be the Lord's adopted child. As a reminder, in the ceremony prescribed for offering the first fruits after entering the Land, the mandatory phrase is included: "My father was a wandering Aramean."[63]

Since Israel is viewed as a foreign child adopted (chosen) by God, she is also viewed as a *ger*. Indeed, the Land belongs to God and He simply bequeaths it to Israel, as His adopted child.

> The land, moreover, shall not be sold permanently, for the land is Mine; for you are but aliens and sojourners with Me. (Leviticus 25:23)

Israel, therefore, could never be confident in herself—in her own ancestry. She was forever dependent upon God, who had adopted her out of her paganism and made her His child forever. Her right to the Land was only maintained in her relationship with her Father through adoption.

This idea of the adoption of Israel must be what underlies Paul's use of the term "adoption as sons," which he lists as one of the privileges of Israel in Romans 9:4.

> ... who are Israelites, to whom belongs the adoption as sons, and the glory and the covenants and the giving of the Torah and the temple service and the promises.

The Torah that governed the life of the native born also governed the life of the *ger* who had attached himself or herself to the God of Israel.

When Paul uses the phrase "adoption as sons," he is emphasizing the corporate election of Israel as God's firstborn son.[64] God as "Father" is revealed to Israel in the context of his "sonship." However, Israel's sonship is a matter of God's grace and not the mere outworking of a natural course of events. Thus, for Paul, even though the nation is currently in a state of unbelief, Israel is still the adopted (and thus rightful) son of God (note the present tense in Romans 9:4, "to whom belongs the adoption," not "belonged"). Paul includes himself in this adoption, for he writes:

> … so that He might redeem those who were under the Torah, that we might receive the adoption as sons. (Galatians 4:5)

Paul sees God's adoption process as not restricted to the physical offspring of Jacob. All of God's chosen ones, whether descendants of Jacob or brought near from the nations, are God's adopted children. He ascribes the "adoption as sons" to Gentile believers as well.[65] Thus, the "adoption as sons" includes both the nation of Israel, who has rejected Yeshua, and the remnant (made up of Jew and non-Jew) who have received Him. Even though Israel as a nation has rejected the Messiah, she retains her adoptive status, for one day she will come to acknowledge Him. In the meantime, the remnant, consisting of both Jew and non-Jew, is the present manifestation of God's adoptive grace, for the remnant behaves as His true son, embracing the Messiah through whom the adoption has been secured.

It should be carefully noted that Paul's metaphor of adoption, based squarely on the adoption motif of the *Tanakh*, was at odds with the prevailing rabbinic view of his day and the subsequent view of rabbinic Judaism. For rather than finding identity in the elective, choosing, adoptive actions of the Almighty, rabbinic Judaism secures its identity through a physical lineage of Jewishness. Paul saw no cause for putting confidence in the flesh.[66] He certainly could have boasted in his pedigree![67] But he boasted rather in the Messiah.[68] He had come to realize that his position in the covenant was never ultimately based upon his Jewishness, but only upon God's gracious election, presented as adoption through the work of Messiah Yeshua.

This speaks directly to the issue at hand. To think that physical lineage or people group identification (Jewishness) could render one son with greater privileges than another is to fly in the face of God's grace and to diminish both the gospel and the price required to secure its blessings. Jewish lineage is important because God has promised to manifest His omnipotent sovereignty through the people descended from Jacob. But in maintaining this promise to Jacob, one need not exclude the non-descendent, for God has also promised to bring the nations within the scope of that same covenant. God has adopted them both! It is only when the Jew and non-Jew live and worship together as equally adopted brothers in the congregation of Yeshua that God's faithfulness and power are manifest as they should be.

Specific Instructions for the *Ger*

Sabbath:

The *ger* who stays with you is to honor the Sabbath in the same way as the native born. He is to cease from his common labors.[69]

Some have suggested that Exodus 31:12–17 ascribes the Sabbath as a covenant sign to only the native born. But this text must be interpreted in light of the initial giving of the Sabbath commandment at Sinai. Since this clearly included the foreigner who was attached to Israel, the designation "children of Israel" in Exodus 31 must include both Jew and non-Jew who were part of the covenant people. Furthermore, since the Sabbath is the sign of the covenant, and since the *ger* is specifically commanded to keep the Sabbath, it follows that he is being treated as a covenant member.

Festivals:

The *ger* is able to observe *Pesach* (Passover) and *Chag HaMatzot* (Festival of Unleavened Bread) as one whose ancestors were redeemed from Egypt.

The *ger* is not allowed to eat leaven during *Chag HaMatzot*, and, like the native born, to do so incurs being cut off from the congregation.[70] Such a penalty presumes the *ger* is a full-fledged member of the congregation.

Likewise, the *ger* who celebrates *Pesach* must be circumcised, and all the males of his household must be circumcised as well.[71] The language of Exodus 12:48 is important. Only after the *ger* and males belonging to him (most likely meaning the males of his family) are marked as covenant members is he able to "draw near … to do it," which must mean "to present his *Pesach* lamb as the prescribed sacrifice" ("drawing near" being sacrificial language). Thus, the *ger* is one who has joined himself to the congregation of Israel on a generational level, for he has not only accepted the commandments of the Torah (witnessed by his circumcision) but he has been faithful to circumcise his children. The text states: "And he will be as a native born," further amplified by "There shall be one Torah for the native born and for the *ger* who sojourns in your midst."

Note that there is no change of ethnic status. The *ger* is still a *ger*, and the native born, a native born. But the *ger* stands in the congregation with the same privileges (participation in the Feast) and responsibilities of the native born (he is not allowed to eat leaven nor is leaven to remain in his house). He did not enter the covenant through becoming circumcised, nor did circumcision transform him into a "native born." Circumcision was simply an act of obedience—receiving the sign of the covenant of which he was a member. He has drawn near to the God of Abraham, Isaac, and Jacob, and as such, he has been united with God's covenant people even as other sojourners joined Israel in her exodus from Egypt.

The *ger* is to observe *Shavuot, Yom Kippur,* and *Sukkot* as well.[72] The pilgrimage festivals are specifically singled out (as well as *Yom Kippur*). This may well be because the pilgrimage festivals were viewed as a summary of the whole festival cycle, beginning with *Pesach* and ending with *Sukkot.* The pilgrimage festivals tie the people to the Land and specifically to Jerusalem, the center of God's activity in the Land.

Sacrifices:

The *ger* was expected to participate in the prescribed sacrifices and to do so by observing all of the commandments given regarding sacrifices.[73] It is obvious, therefore, that the *ger* would also need to observe the laws of purity as well as all the laws the sacrifices required (purifications, guilt offerings, first-fruits offerings, etc.).

The sacrificial service was the high point of Israelite worship. Far from being a peripheral issue, the bringing of sacrifices was the very essence of "drawing near" in the worship of Israel's God. That the *ger* is confirmed in this privilege shows that his status in Israel was equal with the native born in all matters of worship and service.

Other Ordinances:

The *ger* was prohibited from eating blood and from eating meat from an animal that had died or been torn, and doing so would render him unclean.[74] He was prohibited from participating in idolatrous practices and could be put to death for blasphemy.[75] For the *ger*, murder, personal assault, and damages of property drew the attended penalties.[76] The *ger* could be appointed to gather the ashes of the red heifer, and he had equal access to the cities of refuge.[77] In fact, the *ger* was expected to keep all the commandments. At the reading of the Torah on Sukkot, the whole congregation, including the *ger*, was exhorted to keep "all the words of this Torah" (Deuteronomy 31:12). In the renewal of the covenant, as Israel was entering the Land under the leadership of Joshua, the *ger* is included in the company as the blessings and curses are rehearsed, indicating that he was part of the covenant ceremony and therefore stood as a full-fledged covenant member.[78]

We may conclude that the inclusion of the *ger* in every aspect of the covenant is clearly laid out in the *Tanakh*. Far from being excluded from any part of the Torah, the *ger* is expected to receive and obey all of the ordinances, including the Sabbath, Festivals, laws of purity, civil justice, and Tabernacle/Temple worship, including sacrifices. In each case, the Torah that governed the life of the native born also governed the life of the *ger* who had attached himself or herself to the God of Israel.

Conclusion

God promised Abraham that all of the nations would be blessed in his seed. Paul makes it clear that this promise was realized in the Seed of Abraham; that is, Yeshua.[79] From the earliest times, therefore, God called both the physical descendants of Abraham, as well as chosen ones from the nations, to be members of His covenant, sharing equally in the blessings and the responsibilities of that covenant. Those who were "far off" (those from the nations) have been "brought near."

> For the promise is for you and your children and for all who are far off, as many as the Lord our God will call to Himself. (Acts 2:39)

> But now in Messiah Yeshua you who formerly were far off have been brought near by the blood of Messiah. (Ephesians 2:13)

This is in accordance with the message of the prophets who envisioned the ingathering of the nations to worship the God of Abraham, Isaac, and Jacob, not as people outside the covenant, but as full-fledged covenant members.

The Scriptures therefore portray all of the covenant members as adopted children within the family of God who address Him as their Father and who worship and serve Him in accordance with His gracious teaching in righteousness, the Torah. We worship and serve our King together—as one family.

Summary

"The Torah is Only for Jews"

"The Gentile Christian church is the assembly of the faithful from the nations and Messianic Judaism is the proper place for believing Jews."

The vision of the prophets is that the nations would come to Jerusalem to celebrate the feast of Sukkot, the *mo'ed* (appointed time) that consummates the festival cycle (Zechariah 14:16ff). They would worship the God of Israel, sitting together in the *sukkah*. This is not some perfunctory duty, for the nations have come to seek Israel's covenant God, grasping the hem of a Jewish person as an entreaty to learn of Israel's God and enter the covenant. The point of this prophecy is that the Gentiles should "go with" the Jew to learn and to worship, not find their own separate worship and identity. Isaiah also speaks of the foreigner who attaches himself to the Lord and of foreigners who attached themselves to Jacob. In these prophets, the picture is not "equal but separate," as though there were two groups that have equal covenant status but congregate in their own respective places. Rather it is Jew and Gentile together in one place, worshipping in one way, "equal and together," communing in a unified covenant identity. Not two peoples, but one and not two Torahs, but one.

"The Torah was given to the Jews and was only intended for them. It was not meant to be kept by Gentiles."

That the Gentile or *ger* is considered a covenant member, receiving both the privileges and responsibilities of the covenant, is clear from the activities in which he engages and the covenant consequences assigned to him. He participates in the yearly festivals and is required to observe the statutes of the Torah (Deuteronomy 31:12). The *ger* brings sacrifices to the Lord, is not allowed to eat blood (Leviticus 17:11–13), becomes unclean when eating meat from animals dead or torn (Leviticus 17:15), participates in the ritual of the ashes of the red heifer (Numbers 19:10), receives the death penalty for idolatry or cursing God (Leviticus 20:2; 24:16), participates in corporate forgiveness (Numbers 15:26), and may be cut off from the community for defiance against God (Numbers 19:10), which presupposes that he is a full-fledged member of the community.

"Gentiles are part of the covenant of faith though Abraham and Jews are part of the covenant of the Law through Moses."

These two covenants are not separate and distinct, but are woven together in the flow of redemptive history. The covenant given to Abraham, which promised blessing, land, an enduring covenant relationship between the offspring of Abraham and God, and covenant blessing for all the nations, is reaffirmed in the Mosaic covenant and the giving of the Torah. God, in choosing Abraham and his offspring, was forming a people who would be characterized by His own holiness. Thus, the Mosaic covenant, the Torah, is given to bring about that holiness which would, in turn, procure the promised covenant blessings. To the extent that the Abrahamic covenant both envisioned and incorporated the nations, so the Mosaic covenant, the Torah, is given to all covenant members as the divine revelation of God's holiness, written upon the heart of every covenant member, in order to bring about God's blessings in their lives and in the life of the covenant nation.

Study Questions

"The Torah is Only For Jews"

1. Define the word *ger*? Who does it represent in the *Tanakh*? How does it relate to the term *proselyte*? How does Judaism define these two terms? What do you think caused the rabbis to reinterpret the term *ger* to mean *proselyte*?

2. Describe the conversion ritual created by the rabbis for Gentiles to follow in order to be considered a covenant Jew. What is central to this man-made conversion ritual? Does this give a clearer understanding of who Paul is dealing with when he speaks of "the circumcision"?

3. Compare the Abrahamic and Mosaic covenants. What are the differences? What are the similarities? Are the unilateral or bilateral? What do these terms mean?

4. How does the Mosaic covenant build upon the Abrahamic covenant? How are they two sides of the same coin? How is this a picture of justification and sanctification?

5. How does Paul describe the covenant relationship of the Gentile? (Ephesians 3)

6. The *Tanakh* tells us that the nations will seek to be in covenant with God and ask to "go with" the Jew? Can we logically make the jump from not keeping Torah now to keeping it in the future kingdom? (Zechariah 8:23; 14:16; Isaiah 14:1; 56:6-8)

7. Look at the examples of Israel's adoption by God (Leviticus 25:23; Deuteronomy 7:6; Ezekiel 16:1-5) and Ephraim and Manasseh's adoption by Jacob (Genesis 48:5-11). How do these two examples relate to the picture given us by Paul in Romans 9:4 and Galatians 4:5?

8. Does Paul's picture of adoption extend to Gentile believers as well? How was this different from the prevailing rabbinic teachings of his time? (Romans 8:15, 23; Ephesians 1:5)

9. Review the scriptures that give specific instructions to the *ger* or Gentile regarding keeping the Torah. Do these scriptures indicate that the *ger* was exempt from God's requirements for covenant members? What ramifications does this have for us being covenant members with God? (Exodus 12:19, 48; 20:10; 31:12-17; Leviticus 16:29; 17:8, 12-15, 17-18; 20:2; 23:42-43; 24:16-22; Numbers 15:14-16, 29-30; 19:10; 35:15; Deuteronomy 5:14; 16:10-11, 13-14; 31:12)

10. As covenant members with God, what are we to do and how are we to act according to scripture? As adopted sons and daughters are you living according to the Father's commandments?

Endnotes

[1] Ephesians 3:4–6

[2] The "two will become one" language hearkens back to Genesis 2:24. In fact, marriage in First Century Judaism was considered to constitute a "new birth," where both individuals were accredited a new beginning, their former sins being remitted. See y.*Bikkurim* III, 3, 65c–65d; C. G. Montefiore and H. Loewe, *A Rabbinic Anthology* (Schocken, 1974), 210.

[3] Romans 11:11–24

[4] Exodus 19:5, 6; Numbers 23:9; Deuteronomy 32:9; Amos 3:2

[5] Acts 15:28, 29; Galatians. 5:1–6

[6] Romans 3:1; Galatians 2:11–21

[7] Acts 15:1

[8] Galatians 1:6–9

[9] Ephesians 2:13

[10] m.*Avot* 3.14 (Neusner's translation).

[11] Soncino Edition, Midrash Rabbah, Canticles I.15.1, 85.

[12] J. B. Lightfoot, *St. Paul's Epistle to the Galatians* (Draper, 1891), 258.

[13] C. E. B. Cranfield, *St. Paul and the Law* (SJT 17, 1964), 46.

[14] F. F. Bruce, *Commentary on Galatians* (Eerdmans, 1982), 175.

[15] Hans Dieter Betz, *Galatians* (Fortress, 1979), 165.

[16] Romans 7:12, 14.

[17] The *Akedah*, or "Binding of Isaac", is the account in the book of *Genesis* (22:1-19) of Abraham, at the command of God, taking his son, Isaac, to be offered as a sacrifice on Mount Moriah.

[18] Romans 10:4.

[19] I've used the ESV since it follows more closely the word order of the original Greek.

[20] *KB* lists "as far as" for the first meaning of the preposition *ad*, usually translated "until." Also note the similar meaning given for the Greek *achri*, usually translated "until," in *BDAG*.

[21] Acts 7:38, 53; Hebrews 2:2.

[22] Jubilees 1:29–2:1; Philo, *Som.* 1.145; Josephus, *Ant.* xv. 136; *Apoc. Mos.*, preface.

[23] Exodus 20; Deuteronomy 5.

[24] Isaiah 56:3–5, 7.

[25] Zechariah 8:23.

[26] Isaiah 40:2; Jeremiah 23:5–8; Zechariah 9:12.

[27] Isaiah 44:3; Zechariah 12:10; Jeremiah 31:31–34.

[28] John 10:16; see also Mattthew 10:6; 15:24.

[29] *Eschaton* literally means "being the farthest boundary, last" and is used here to refer to the "last days" or "end of times."

[30] Romans 11:26.

[31] *KB, "ger."*

[32] The only distinction is that of land ownership via ancestral lineage for the native born.

[33] *The Stone Chumash* (Mesorah Pub., 1993).

[34] It is also not found in the *Mishnah*, indicating that its acceptance as a technical term was in the post-Mishnaic period.

[35] m.*Sanhedrin* 10:1, cf. b.*Sanhedrin* 90a.

[36] *Sarah*, "to contend" or "to fight" and *El*, "God"; thus the common understanding is "He who contends with God." Others have suggested "God fights," "God rules," and "God heals"; cf. *KB, "Israel."*

[37] Used 637 times in the *Tanakh*, the expression, which began as a designation of the physical sons of Jacob, soon became the title for the whole nation.

[38] This is obvious by the fact that Exodus 13:2 speaks of the "wombs" among the "sons of Israel." Furthermore, the "sons of Israel" all passed through the Red Sea on dry ground (Exodus 14:22) and all ate the manna (Exodus 16:35). In Exodus 35:29, the "sons of Israel" are specifically defined as "all the men and women" who brought offerings for the building of the Tabernacle.

[39] Exodus 12:19, 48; 20:10; 22:21; 23:9,12; Leviticus 16:29; 17:8, 10; 18:26; 19:10, 34; 20:2; 22:18; 23:22; 24:16, 22; Numbers 9:14; 15:14–16,26,29–30; 19:10; 35:15; Deuteronomy 1:16; 5:14; 10:19; 14:29; 16:11, 14; 24:14, 17, 19--21; 26:11–13; 27:19; 31:12; Joshua 8:33, 35; Isaiah 14:1; Jeremiah 7:6; 22:3; Ezekiel 14:7; 22:7, 29; Zechariah 7:10; Malachi 3:5.

[40] Weekly Sabbath, Exodus 20:10; Deuteronomy 5:14; Pesach, Exodus 12:48, 49; Numbers 9:14; Feast of Unleavened Bread, Exodus 12:19; Shavuot, Deuteronomy 16:10, 11, cf. Deuteronomy 26:10, 11; Yom Kippur, Leviticus 16:29; Sukkot, Deuteronomy 16:13, 14, but cf. Leviticus 23:42.

[41] Leviticus 17:8; 22:18; Num 9:14; 15:14.

[42] Genesis 12:3; 18:18; 22:18; 26:4; 28:14.

[43] There are, of course, stipulations connected with the Abrahamic covenant; i.e., circumcision. But the failure to circumcise affects the individual, not the whole nation. The structure of the Abrahamic covenant clearly follows that of the Royal Grant Treaty, which is unilateral, not bilateral as the Suzerain-Vassal treaty is. There is little doubt that, though there may be matters of reciprocity in the Abrahamic covenant (as is the case in all covenants), the major thrust of the narrative structure in which the Abrahamic covenant is given is that it is a unilateral covenant dependent upon God's faithfulness, not Abraham's.

[44] Ruth 2:12; Psalms 61:4.

[45] Deuteronomy 23:3

[46] Deuteronomy 16:11; 26:11; 28:43; 29:11; Joshua 8:35.

[47] Ephesians 2:11-13.

[48] E.g., Leviticus 1:2–3, 5,10,13–14; 2:11–12; 3:1, 7, 12; 6:20; 7:11; 9:2

[49] Note, for example, 1 Samuel 14:36.

[50] Ephesians 3:6. The compound words are all constructed with the Greek preposition *sun*, meaning "with" or "together with"; *sugkleronomos, sussomos, summetochos.* These emphasize vital union and sharing of things held in common.

[51] Galatians 3:8.

[52] Isaiah 56:7.

[53] *Halachah* is a Hebrew word meaning "to walk." The term is used to describe how an individual "walks" out the scriptures in their life. This of course varies from person to person; sect to sect and community to community.

[54] Matthew 8:11.

[55] The hem of a garment had clear covenant connection in the ancient Near East. See my article, "Hem, Covenant and 1 Samuel" available at *www.torahresource.com.* It is also a common reference to the *tzitzit* or fringes attached to the four corners on the hem of a garment.

[56] Isaiah 14:1; 56:6–8.

[57] Exodus 12:19; Leviticus 16:29; 17:15; 18:26; 24:16; Numbers 9:14; 15:16; 29–30.

[58] Acts 13:32ff.

[59] Note the remarks of J. J. Rabinowitz, "Semitic Elements in the Egyptian Adoption Papyrus Published by Gardiner," *JNES* 17(1958), 145–46.

[60] Genesis 18:19 uses the Hebrew word *yada*, "to know" in the sense of "covenant relationship." "For I have chosen him" is literally, "For I have known him." Cf. Amos 3:2, "You only have I known (chosen) among all the families of the earth."

[61] See the comments of Nahum Sarna, *The JPS Torah Commentary: Genesis* (JPS, 1989), 207.

[62] Ezekiel 16:1-5.

[63] Deuteronomy 26:5.

[64] Exodus 4:22ff; Jeremiah 31:9; Hosea 11:1.

[65] Romans 8:15, 23; Ephesians 1:5.

[66] Philippians 3:3. Paul's use of the word *flesh* in certain contexts almost certainly means "relying upon one's physical lineage and connection to the Jewish community."

[67] 2 Corinthians 11:18–22; Phillippians 3:4–6.

[68] 2 Corinthians 12:9; Galatians 6:13–14.

[69] Exodus 20:10; Deuteronomy 5:14.

[70] Exodus 12:19.

[71] Exodus 12:48.

[72] Deuteronomy 16:10–11, 13–14; Leviticus 16:29. Leviticus 23:42–43 specifically details Sukkot as for the "native-born" but it cannot negate the requirement of Deuteronomy that the *ger* should celebrate the festival as well. It only highlights the fact that the *ger* is to function in every way as the native born.

[73] Leviticus 17:8; 22:17–18; Numbers 15:14–16.

[74] Leviticus 17:12–13, 15. It may appear that Deuteronomy 14:21 contradicts this, for it allows the *ger* to eat the torn meat. But the context indicates that in this case the word *ger* must mean a foreigner who is passing through Israel and has not attached himself to Israel through faith in her God. The subsequent clause has "or sell it to a foreigner (*nochri*)," a term used most often of pagans.

[75] Leviticus 24:16; 20:2; Numbers 15:29–30.

[76] Leviticus 24:17–22

[77] Numbers 19:10; 35:15; Joshua 20:9.

[78] Joshua 8:33–35.

[79] Galatians 3:16ff.